Logic Thinker Sheets

by

Becky Daniel

illustrated by Nancee McClure

Cover by Nancee McClure

ISBN No. 0-86653-505-5

Printing No. 987654321

GOOD APPLE, INC.
1204 BUCHANAN ST., BOX 299
CARTHAGE, IL 62321-0299

Dedication

For my dad,
who dreams of building by night
and builds his dreams by day.

Table of Contents

To the Teacher

Webster's Dictionary defines *logic* as "correct reasoning; sound thinking; the science that deals with the rules of correct reasoning and with proof by reasoning; a way of reasoning." One of the first steps for children in the process of deductive reasoning is for them to put pencil to paper and list the possible solutions of a problem. For this reason, most of the puzzles in this book provide a chart of possibilities. Learners simply cross off the possibilities that are contradicted by the facts, leaving the only remaining possibility and correct answer. A few puzzles require children to construct their own charts. These charts may be constructed in many ways. They may be very long and involved, listing every possibility, or the charts may incorporate some of the facts, thus limiting the number of possibilities from the start. Discussions regarding quicker solutions should be encouraged. When time allows, have children create their own abbreviated possibility charts to share with peers.

Logic Thinker Sheets will give children an opportunity to sharpen their deductive reasoning skills. When working these puzzles, children are required to recognize certain facts and deduce conclusions based on reasoning. The wide range of activities, from simple to complex, will give learners concrete practice in logical thinking that they may never otherwise receive. Many school-aged children spend most of their time in programs that emphasize simple recall and memorization of facts rather than higher thinking and reasoning. The activities in this book require children not only to deduce answers from given possibilities, but will also provide a framework for them to more easily move through the deductive process. Often answers will vary.

Encourage students to discuss answers with classmates, parents and other adults. Working in a group with a given time limit is another good way to use the activities in this book. Remember, the thinking process is more important than finding the solution, but don't deny children the satisfaction of arriving at an acceptable answer.

Each page contains a bonus. These activities are usually very difficult and should not be a requirement. Use the bonus activities for extra credit. Students that complete one of these should receive special recognition. A class competition could involve keeping track of how many bonus activities are completed by each student and rewarding those that complete a given number. Awards are found on pages 59 and 60 and a special award certificate for bonus activities is included. For review, have the children follow up some of the activity pages by creating their own facts that will deduce a new conclusion. When possible, have students verbalize the steps they followed to reach their conclusions. Don't be surprised if soon you find you have a whole classroom full of young Aristotles!

Beautiful, Blond and Intelligent

There are four sisters named Virginia, Wendy, Yvette and Zelda. Several are beautiful, several are intelligent, each has red, brown or blond hair. Only one is beautiful, blond and intelligent. Use the facts and complete the chart found below to deduce which sister is beautiful, blond and intelligent.

Facts:

1. The only two sisters with red hair are standing on either side of Yvette.
2. On either side of Wendy are standing the only two intelligent sisters, or Virginia is beautiful.
3. Wendy and Yvette have the same hair color and Virginia is blond, or Zelda and Yvette are the only two beautiful sisters and Virginia has brown hair.

Virginia
Wendy
Yvette
Zelda

	Virginia	Wendy	Yvette	Zelda
Beautiful				
Hair Color				
Intelligent				

Answer:

Bonus: Which sister is not blond, beautiful or intelligent?

Name ______________________________

Let's Dine Out!

Three couples named Brown, White and Green dined together. Use the facts and diagram found below to deduce the seating arrangement of the couples around the table.

Facts:

1. Either each husband sat on the left of his wife or directly across the table from her.
2. Either Mr. Green or Mrs. Green sat directly across the table from Mrs. Brown.

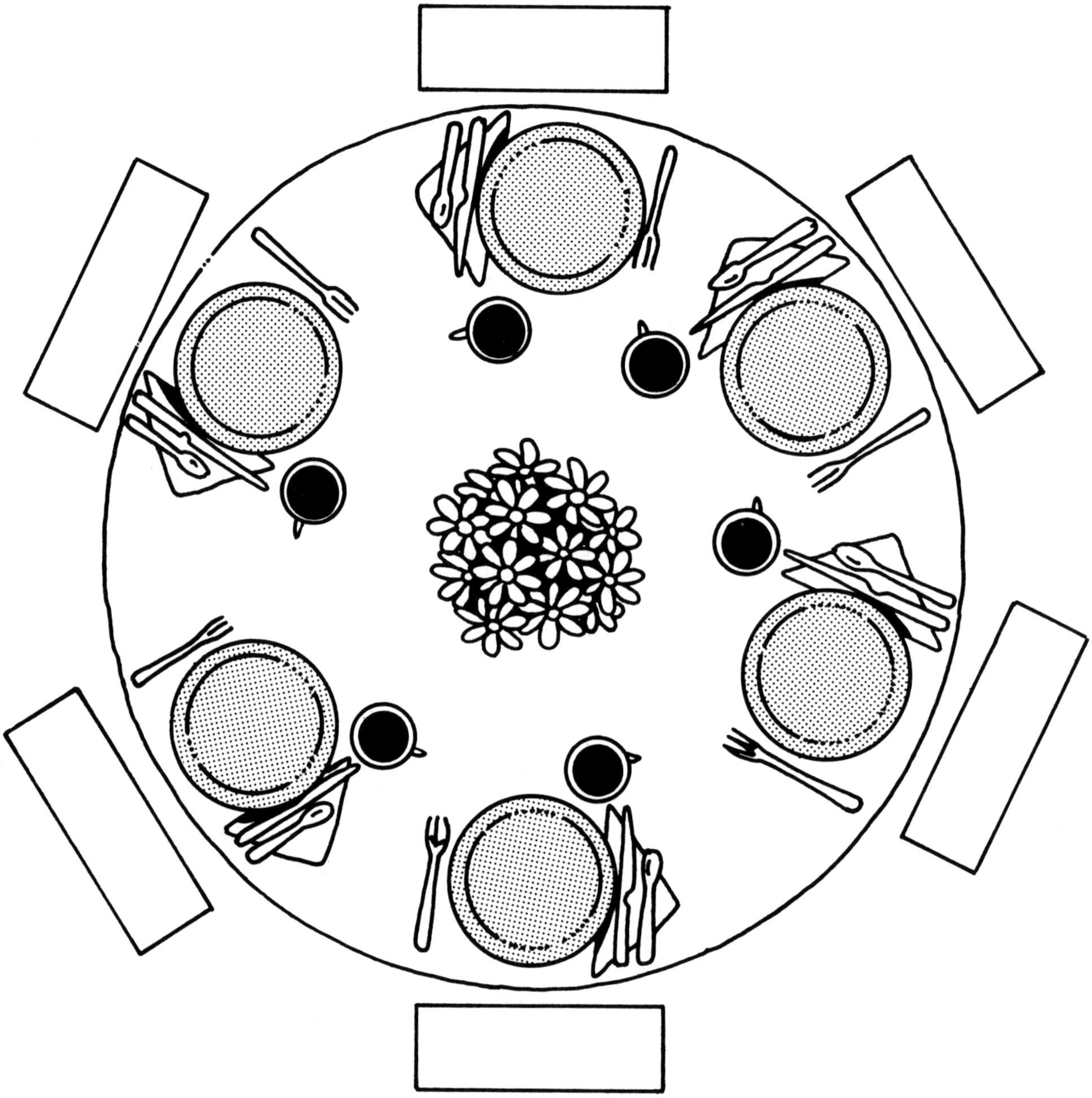

Bonus: Is it possible to draw a diagram showing a seating arrangement so that no husband sits next to or directly across from his wife?

Name ____________________

What's My Line?

A man named Mike has a mother, wife and son. Mike or one of his relatives is a doctor, lawyer, teacher or writer. Use the facts and complete the chart found below to deduce the occupation of each person. (Cross out each possibility that contradicts the facts. You will be left with the only possibility.)

Facts:

1. The lawyer and doctor are both men or both women.
2. The teacher and writer are father and son or husband and wife.
3. The writer and lawyer are husband and wife or grandmother and grandson.
4. Mike is not married to the doctor.

MIKE/DOCTOR	WIFE/LAWYER	SON/TEACHER	MOTHER/WRITER
MIKE/DOCTOR	WIFE/TEACHER	SON/LAWYER	MOTHER/WRITER
MIKE/DOCTOR	WIFE/LAWYER	SON/WRITER	MOTHER/TEACHER
MIKE/DOCTOR	WIFE/TEACHER	SON/WRITER	MOTHER/LAWYER
MIKE/DOCTOR	WIFE/WRITER	SON/TEACHER	MOTHER/LAWYER
MIKE/DOCTOR	WIFE/WRITER	SON/LAWYER	MOTHER/TEACHER
MIKE/LAWYER	WIFE/WRITER	SON/DOCTOR	MOTHER/TEACHER
MIKE/LAWYER	WIFE/WRITER	SON/TEACHER	MOTHER/DOCTOR
MIKE/LAWYER	WIFE/TEACHER	SON/DOCTOR	MOTHER/WRITER
MIKE/LAWYER	WIFE/TEACHER	SON/WRITER	MOTHER/DOCTOR
MIKE/LAWYER	WIFE/DOCTOR	SON/TEACHER	MOTHER/WRITER
MIKE/LAWYER	WIFE/DOCTOR	SON/WRITER	MOTHER/TEACHER
MIKE/WRITER	WIFE/TEACHER	SON/DOCTOR	MOTHER/LAWYER
MIKE/WRITER	WIFE/TEACHER	SON/LAWYER	MOTHER/DOCTOR
MIKE/WRITER	WIFE/DOCTOR	SON/TEACHER	MOTHER/LAWYER
MIKE/WRITER	WIFE/DOCTOR	SON/LAWYER	MOTHER/TEACHER
MIKE/WRITER	WIFE/LAWYER	SON/TEACHER	MOTHER/DOCTOR
MIKE/WRITER	WIFE/LAWYER	SON/DOCTOR	MOTHER/TEACHER
MIKE/TEACHER	WIFE/LAWYER	SON/DOCTOR	MOTHER/WRITER
MIKE/TEACHER	WIFE/LAWYER	SON/WRITER	MOTHER/DOCTOR
MIKE/TEACHER	WIFE/DOCTOR	SON/WRITER	MOTHER/LAWYER
MIKE/TEACHER	WIFE/DOCTOR	SON/LAWYER	MOTHER/WRITER
MIKE/TEACHER	WIFE/WRITER	SON/LAWYER	MOTHER/DOCTOR
MIKE/TEACHER	WIFE/WRITER	SON/DOCTOR	MOTHER/LAWYER

Answer:

Bonus: What percent of the possibilities are eliminated by fact number one?

Name ______________________

A Triple Date

Three boys named Tom, Tim and Eric are dating three girls named Betty, Beth and Jamie. Use the facts and the chart found below to deduce which boy is dating which girl.

Facts:

1. Eric is dating Betty and Tim is dating Jamie, or Eric is dating Jamie and Tom is dating Betty.
2. Tom is dating Betty and Eric is dating Jamie, or Tom is dating Beth and Tim is dating Betty.

ERIC/BETTY	TOM/BETH	TIM/JAMIE
ERIC/BETTY	TOM/JAMIE	TIM/BETH
ERIC/BETH	TOM/BETTY	TIM/JAMIE
ERIC/BETH	TOM/JAMIE	TIM/BETTY
ERIC/JAMIE	TOM/BETH	TIM/BETTY
ERIC/JAMIE	TOM/BETTY	TIM/BETH

Answer:

Bonus: If the only fact given had read, "Tom is dating Jamie and Eric is dating Beth, or Tom is dating Beth and Eric is dating Jamie," could you name one couple?

Name ____________________

Hawaii Bound

The tallest and the oldest of three sisters named Naomi, Linda and Diane are going to Hawaii for a vacation. Use the facts and complete the chart found below to deduce which two sisters are going to Hawaii. (It may be easier to note what is not possible first and then go back and figure out what possibilities are left open.)

Facts:

1. Naomi is the youngest and Diane is the tallest, or Naomi is the oldest and Diane is the shortest.
2. Linda is the tallest and the youngest, or she is the shortest and the oldest.
3. Diane is the middle sister in height and Naomi is the oldest, or Diane is the middle sister in age and Naomi is the youngest.

	Oldest	Middle	Youngest	Shortest	Middle	Tallest
Naomi						
Linda						
Diane						

Answer:

Bonus: If next summer the youngest and the shortest sisters go to Hawaii, which sister will visit the islands twice?

Name ____________________

Four Friends

Four children named Nancy, Kathy, Dave and Jay help their teacher after school. Each day a different pair of children stayed. Use the facts and complete the chart found below to deduce which two children helped the teacher each day after school. (Cross off the boxes that contradict the facts.)

Facts:

1. Neither of the girls ever stayed to help the teacher two days in a row.
2. On Monday, Kathy and Nancy stayed to help, or Jay and Nancy stayed to help.
3. On Friday, Kathy and David stayed to help or Kathy and Jay stayed to help.
4. On Monday the helpers were both boys or both girls.
5. On Wednesday, Kathy and David stayed to help, or David and Jay stayed to help.
6. Jay could not stay on Thursday, or Kathy could not stay on Friday.

	Mon.	Tues.	Wed.	Thurs.	Fri.
Kathy & Nancy					
Kathy & David					
Kathy & Jay					
David & Jay					
David & Nancy					
Nancy & Jay					

Answer:

Bonus: If fact 1 wasn't given, could this puzzle be solved with the other facts given?

Name ____________________

Last Name, Please

Three girls named Kathy, Carole and Helen went to a party. Use the facts and the chart below to deduce the last name of each girl. (Cross off the possibilities that contradict the facts and you will be left with the only possibility.)

Facts:

1. Kathy came in just before Miss Evans.
2. Carole's last name is Evans if Helen's last name is Mac, or Carole's last name is Mac if Helen's last name is Evans.
3. Miss Mac spoke briefly to Helen at the end of the party.

1.	KATHY JOE	HELEN MAC	CAROLE EVANS
2.	KATHY JOE	CAROLE MAC	HELEN EVANS
3.	KATHY MAC	HELEN JOE	CAROLE EVANS
4.	KATHY MAC	CAROLE JOE	HELEN EVANS
5.	KATHY EVANS	HELEN JOE	CAROLE MAC
6.	KATHY EVANS	CAROLE JOE	HELEN MAC

Answer:

Bonus: If fact 3 was changed to read, "Miss Evans spoke briefly to Helen as the party was ending," who came in just before Miss Joe at the party?

Name ______________________

What's for Lunch, Boys?

Three boys named Adam, Bob and Carl ate lunch together. Use the facts and complete the chart found below to deduce what each boy ate and drank for lunch. (Cross off each possibility contradicted by a fact, and you will be left with the clues you need to deduce the answer.)

Hint: No boy ate or drank the same thing.

Facts:

1. Adam drank a soda and Bob had a shake, or Carl had the soda and Adam had the shake.
2. Carl had salad and Adam had a burger, or Carl had a burger and Adam had pizza.
3. The boy that ate a burger drank milk or soda.
4. Bob had the pizza and a shake, or he had a burger and milk.
5. Adam hates pizza, and he never drinks milk.

	Adam	Bob	Carl
Burger/Milk			
Burger/Shake			
Burger/Soda			
Pizza/Milk			
Pizza/Shake			
Pizza/Soda			
Salad/Milk			
Salad/Shake			
Salad/Soda			

Answer:

Bonus: If fact 5 was changed to read "Bob and Carl are vegetarians," what did each boy have for lunch?

Name ____________________

The Dating Game

Three boys named Curly, Larry and Moe went on a blind date with triplets named Anna, Anita, and Andrea. After the date, the boys asked the girls their names. Use the facts and construct and complete a chart to deduce which boy dated which girl.

Facts:

1. Andrea said, "You were with me, Larry, and Anita was with Curly; or Anita was with you, Larry, and Anna was with Curly."
2. Anita said, "Moe was with my sister, Anna, and I was with Curly; or Moe was with me, and Larry was with Anna."

Answer:

Bonus: If Anna said, "No, Andrea, you have it all wrong! Larry was with you and Curly was with Anita, or Moe was with you and Larry was with Anita," who is dating whom?

Name ____________________

No Clowning Around

A diamond ring was stolen from Mrs. Price's dressing table during her annual Halloween costume party. Mr. Price saw the guest dressed like a clown leaving the bedroom just before the ring disappeared. In all the confusion, Mrs. Price can only remember three facts. Use the facts to construct and complete a chart to deduce which guest should be held for questioning.

Facts:

1. Mr. Red and Mrs. Red came as a devil and an angel respectively, or Mr. White and Mrs. White wore the devil and angel costumes.
2. Mr. Sue was dressed like a ladybug or a devil, and his wife was dressed like an angel or William Shakespeare.
3. Mr. Red wore the lion costume and Mrs. White wore the ladybug costume, or Mr. Red wore a devil costume and Mr. White wore the lion costume.

Answer:

Bonus: If the last fact was changed to read, "Mr. Red wore the Shakespeare costume and Mrs. White was the ladybug, or Mr. Red wore the devil costume and Mrs. White wore the lion's costume," who is the suspect?

Name ____________________

They All Have Wheels

Three boys named Chris, Victor and Brad each used a different form of transportation. Use the facts to construct a chart to deduce the mode of transportation each boy used.

Facts:

1. Chris rode his bike and Brad skated, or Brad rode his bike and Chris skated.
2. Chris rode his bike and Victor took a scooter, or Brad rode his bike and Victor skated.

Answer:

Bonus: Create a puzzle with three girls named Flo, Fauna, and Fern who collect rocks, shells and glass horses. You may include only two facts. Draw a chart to prove your puzzle can be solved.

Name ____________________

What Color Hat?

There are two children named Beth and John. There are three hats; two are blue and one is orange. Each child is wearing a hat. Neither child can see his/her own hat or the hat that is unworn. Each child can see only the hat worn by the other child. Use the facts and complete the chart found below to deduce the color of Beth's hat.

Facts:

1. After looking at Beth's hat, John said, "I do not know the color of my hat."
2. After looking at John's hat, Beth said, "I do know the color of my hat."

What the children would say if. . .	**Fact 1**	**Fact 2**
John/Blue and Beth/Blue	?	
John/Orange and Beth/Blue		
John/Blue and Beth/Orange		

Answer:

Bonus: If John's hat was orange, explain how Beth would know the color of her hat. If John's hat was blue, explain how Beth might be able to deduce the color of her hat.

Name ________________________

Five Hats

There are three children named Amy, Sarah and Eric. There are five hats; two are yellow and three are pink. Each child can see only two hats, those worn by the other children. The children cannot see the unworn hats or their own hats. Use the fact and complete the chart found below to deduce the color of each child's hat.

Fact:

1. When asked if any of the children knew the color of their own hats, Eric was the only one that knew the color of his hat.

What the children would say if. . .	Amy	Sarah	Eric
Amy/Pink Sarah/Pink Eric/Pink	?	?	?
Amy/Yellow Sarah/Pink Eric/Pink			
Amy/Yellow Sarah/Yellow Eric/Pink			
Amy/Pink Sarah/Yellow Eric/Yellow			
Amy/Pink Sarah/Yellow Eric/Pink			
Amy/Pink Sarah/Pink Eric/Yellow			
Amy/Yellow Sarah/Pink Eric/Yellow			

Answer:

Bonus: If Amy, wearing a yellow hat, said, "I do not know the color of my hat," and Sarah, wearing a pink hat, said, "I do not know the color of my hat either," and Eric said he knew the color of his hat, how did he know?

Name ______________________________

Black and White Hats

There are three children named Mike, Max and Nancy. There are five hats, three black and two white. Each child can see only two hats, those worn by the other children. Use the facts and construct a chart to deduce the color of Nancy's hat.

Facts:

1. After looking at the other children's hats, Mike said, "I don't know the color of my hat."
2. After looking at the other children's hats, Max said, "I don't know the color of my hat either."
3. After looking at the other children's hats, Nancy said, "I know the color of my hat."

Answer:

Bonus: If none of the three children could name the color of their hats, what color are they wearing?

Name ____________________

GA1099

Six Hats

There are three girls named Julie, Jill and Janet. There are six hats, three red and three green. Each girl can see only the two hats worn by the other girls. The girls cannot see their own hats or the unworn hats. Use the facts and complete the chart found below to deduce the color of Julie's hat.

Facts:

1. When asked if they could see a red hat, all three girls answered, "Yes."
2. When asked if they could name the color of their hats, Julie was the only girl that said she could.

What each girl would say if. . .	Jill	Janet	Julie
JILL/RED JANET/RED JULIE/RED	?	?	?
JILL/RED JANET/RED JULIE/GREEN			
JILL/RED JANET/GREEN JULIE/RED			
JILL/GREEN JANET/RED JULIE/RED			

Answer:

Bonus: If Janet and Julie had both said they could name the color of their hats, and then Jill had said, "If my sisters know the color of their hats, then I can deduce the color of mine," what color hat is each sister wearing?

Name ______________________

The Prize Box

There are two boxes. One box contains a prize and the other box is empty. Each box has a note attached to it. One of the notes is a true statement, and one is a false statement. Complete the chart found below to deduce which box contains the prize.

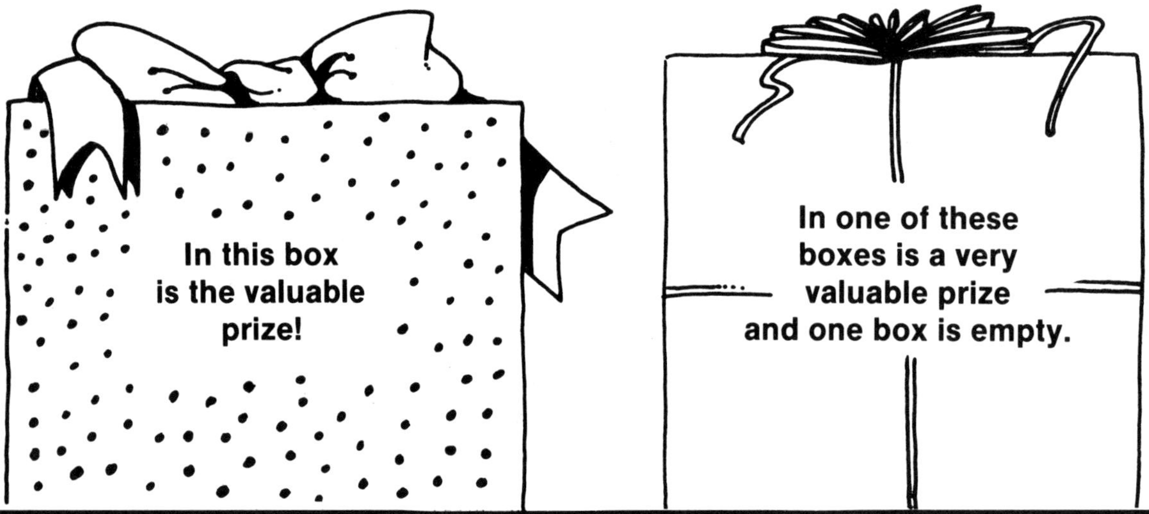
In this box is the valuable prize!
In one of these boxes is a very valuable prize and one box is empty.

What's inside if. . .	Box 1	Box 2
Box 1/True Box 2/False		
Box 1/False Box 2/True		

Answer:

Bonus: If both of the notes on the boxes are true or both of the notes are false, which box contains the prize?

Name ____________________

Three Boxes

There are three boxes. One box contains a prize and the other two boxes are empty. Each box has a note attached to it. Only one of the three notes is true. The other two notes are both false. Complete the chart to deduce which box contains the prize.

This box is empty.
This box contains the prize. The first box is empty.
This box is empty. Choose another one.

What's inside if. . .	Box 1	Box 2	Box 3
Box 1/True Box 2/False Box 3/False			
Box 1/False Box 2/True Box 3/False			
Box 1/False Box 2/False Box 3/True			

Answer:

Bonus: If the notes attached to each box are all true or all false, which box contains the prize?

Name ______________________

All True or All Lies

There are three boxes. One contains a prize and two are empty. Each box has a note attached to it. Either the notes attached to the boxes are all true or all false. Construct a chart to deduce which box contains the prize.

This box contains the prize.
This box is empty.
This box contains the prize.

Answer:

Bonus: If one note is true, one is false and the other note may or may not be true, which box will you definitely NOT choose? Can you deduce which box contains the prize?

Name ______________________

Pick a Box, Any Box!

There are four boxes. One box contains a prize and the other three boxes are empty. Each box has a note attached to it. One note is completely false. The other three notes are completely true. Complete the chart found below to deduce which box contains the prize.

CRUNCHOS
LOOK inside! The prize is in this box.
This box is empty and so is the fourth box.
ZINGERS
WOWS
This box is empty. The prize is in the first box.
The note on box one is completely false. This box contains the prize.
NUTS

What's inside if...	Box 1	Box 2	Box 3	Box 4
F/T/T/T	E/P	E	E	E/P
T/F/T/T				
T/T/F/T				
T/T/T/F				

Answer:

Bonus: Make up your own box puzzle with two true clues and two false clues.

Name ____________________

Say That Again

There are four boxes. Inside one box is a prize and the other three boxes are empty. Each box has a note attached to it. One note is completely false. The other three notes contain completely true statements. Draw a chart to deduce which box contains the prize.

The prize is inside this box, and the fourth box is empty.
This box is empty, and the prize is in the fourth box.
This box is empty, and the second box is also empty.
The prize is inside this box, and the first box is empty.

Answer:

Bonus: If the word *and* is changed on all four boxes to read *or* and all the statements are true, construct a chart to deduce where the prize might be.

Name ______________________

George's Rabbits

There is a boy named George, who has three rabbits. One rabbit is black, one rabbit is white, and one rabbit is spotted. Each rabbit is in a covered box. Each box has a note attached to it. Two notes are false and one is true. After peeking inside the first box, George said, "The spotted rabbit is in the third box." Complete the chart to deduce the color of rabbit George saw in the first box.

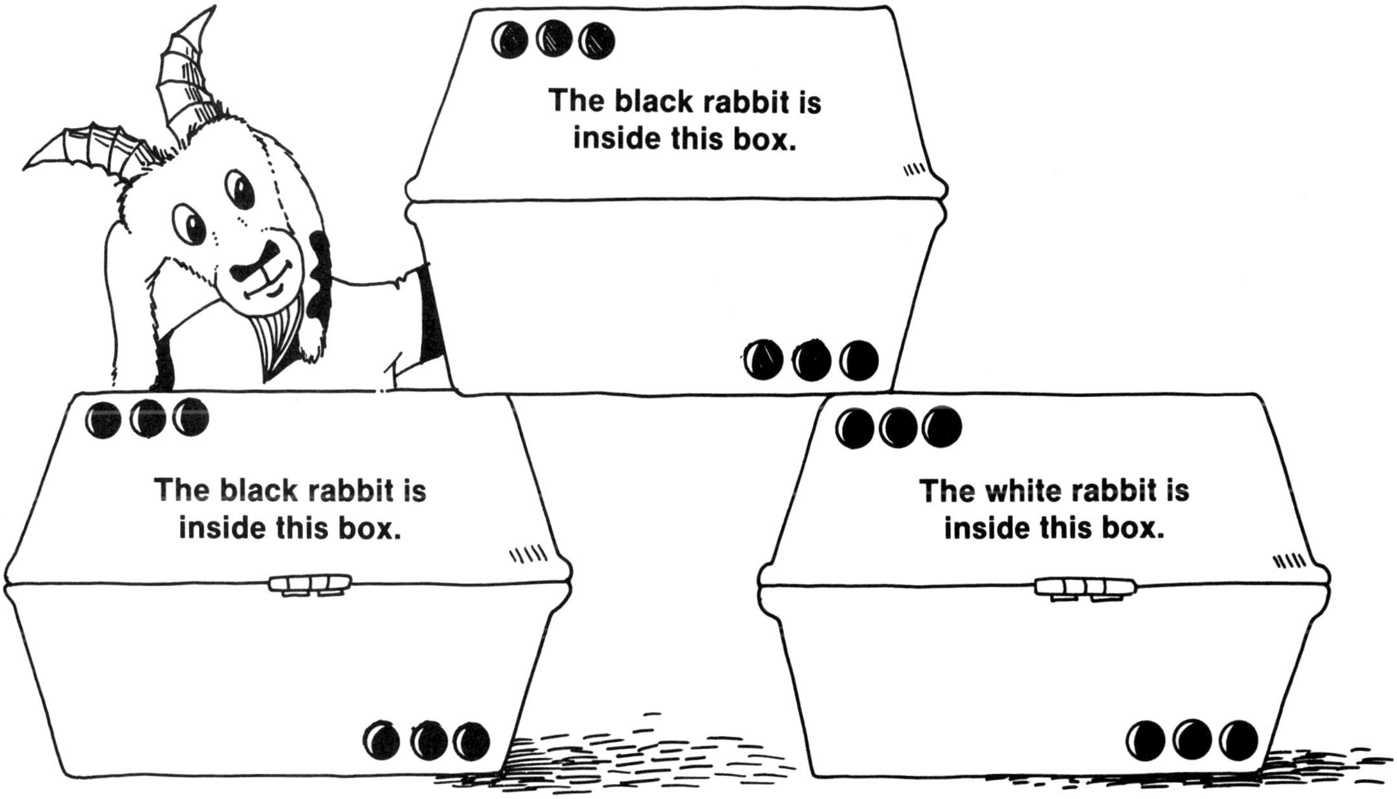

The black rabbit is inside this box.
The black rabbit is inside this box.
The white rabbit is inside this box.

What's inside if George sees . . .	Box 1	Box 2	Box 3
Black			
White			

Answer:

Bonus: If all three statements are false and George looks in the first box and says, "Here is the spotted rabbit," what color rabbit is in box two?

Name ____________________

Suzi's Rabbits

There is a girl named Suzi, who has three rabbits. One rabbit is gray, one rabbit is brown, and one rabbit is white. Each rabbit is in a covered box. Each box has a note attached to it. Two of the notes are false, and one of the notes is true. After peeking inside the first box, Suzi said, "I see the brown rabbit." Construct a chart to deduce what color rabbit is in each remaining box.

The white rabbit is inside this box.
The brown rabbit is inside this box.
The gray rabbit is inside this box.

Answer:

Bonus: If Suzi had peeked inside the second box instead of the first box and had said she saw a gray rabbit, which box contains the brown rabbit?

Name ______________________________

Pete's Rabbits

There is a boy named Pete, who has four rabbits. One rabbit is black, one rabbit is white, one rabbit is gray, and one rabbit is brown. Each rabbit is in a covered box. Each box has a note attached to it. Three of the notes are true and one note is false. Pete looked inside the last box and said, "The gray rabbit is in the first box." Can you deduce the color of the rabbit in each of the other boxes?

Answer:

The black rabbit is inside this box.
The brown rabbit is inside this box.
The white rabbit is inside this box.
The black rabbit is inside this box.

Bonus: Write your own rabbit-in-box puzzle.

Name ______________________________

Bryan's Rabbits

There is a boy named Bryan, who has four rabbits. One rabbit is black, one rabbit is brown, one rabbit is gray and one rabbit is white. Each rabbit is in a covered box. Each box has a note attached to it. Two of the notes contain completely true statements, and two of the notes contain completely false statements. Bryan looked inside the first box and saw a brown rabbit. Can you deduce what color rabbit is in each of the remaining boxes?

Inside this box is a brown rabbit. The black rabbit is in the last box.
Inside this box is a gray rabbit. The last box contains the brown rabbit.
Inside this box is a gray rabbit. The white rabbit is inside the second box.
Inside this box is a brown rabbit. The black rabbit is inside the first box.

Answer:

Bonus: If Bryan had looked inside the second box instead of the first box and saw a gray rabbit, which box contains the white rabbit?

Name ____________________________

Barbara and Joann

There are identical twins named Barbara and Joann. One sister always tells the truth and one sister always lies. You do not know the name of the truth-teller or the name of the liar, and you cannot tell the sisters apart. Use the facts and complete the chart found below to deduce which sister you are addressing.

Facts:

1. When asked if her name was Barbara, the girl answered, "Yes."
2. When asked if Barbara is a truth-teller, the girl again answered, "Yes."

If you are speaking to. . .	Reply to Question 1	Reply to Question 2
Barbara/ Truth-teller		
Barbara/Liar		
Joann/Truth-teller		
Joann/Liar		

Answer:

Bonus: On a different day, you again meet a twin. You ask her only one question. She answers the question, "Yes." You know which sister you are addressing and whether she is the truth-teller or liar. What question did you ask her?

Name ____________________

You Decide

There are two men named Lee and George. One is a doctor and the other is the patient. One man always tells the truth, and the other man always lies. You question both of the men and discover three facts. Use the facts and complete the chart found below to deduce who is the doctor and who is the patient. Who is the truth-teller and who is the liar?

Facts:

1. Lee said that George is the doctor.
2. George said that Lee is the doctor.
3. Lee said that the doctor is a liar.

If. . .	**Fact 1**	**Fact 2**	**Fact 3**
Lee Truth-teller/Doctor and George Liar/Patient			
Lee Liar/Doctor and George Truth-teller/Patient			
Lee Truth-teller/Patient and George Liar/Doctor			
Lee Liar/Patient and George Truth-teller/Doctor			

Answer:

Bonus: If fact 3 read, "George said that the doctor is a liar," would the doctor still be a liar? What would be the name of the patient?

Name ______________________________

Arrest That Twin!

There are identical twin brothers named Peter and Paul. One brother never tells the truth. The other brother tells the truth sometimes and lies sometimes. Paul committed a crime and must be arrested. Use the facts and complete the chart found below to deduce which brother is Paul and should be arrested. Is Paul the first speaker or the second speaker?

Facts:

1. When asked if he was Peter, the first man said, "Yes."
2. When asked if he was Peter, the second man said, "No."

If. . .	Reply to Question 1	Reply to Question 2
Peter/Truth Paul/Lying		
Peter/Lying Paul/Lying		
Peter/Lying Paul/Truth		
Paul/Truth Peter/Lying		
Paul/Lying Peter/Truth		
Paul/Lying Peter/Lying		

Answer:

Bonus: If the second speaker had claimed to be Peter instead of the first speaker, which one is Paul?

Name ____________________

Double Whammy

There are four brothers named Tom, Jeff, Doug, and Jack. You have never met the brothers so you do not know what they look like. You do know that Tom is an accurate truth-teller. Jeff is an inaccurate truth-teller (he thinks the opposite is truth so always states a lie). Doug is an accurate liar (knows the truth and always states the opposite). Jack is an inaccurate liar (both deluded and dishonest). You meet and speak to one of the brothers. Use the facts and complete the chart found below to deduce which brother you are addressing.

Facts:

1. When asked if he is a truth-teller, the brother answered, "Yes."
2. When asked if he is Jack, the brother answered, "Yes."

	Fact #1 Answer	**Fact #2 Answer**
Tom, Accurate Truth-teller		
Jeff, Inaccurate Truth-teller		
Doug, Accurate Liar		
Jack, Inaccurate Liar		

Answer:

Bonus: Which brother would answer "Yes," if asked, "Are you Doug?"

Name ____________________

Willard and Gene

There are identical twin brothers named Willard and Gene. You cannot tell the brothers apart, but you do know that one brother always tells the truth, and one brother always lies. You do not know the name of the truth-teller or the name of the liar. Use the facts below and construct and complete a chart to deduce which brother you are addressing.

Facts:

1. When asked if his name is Willard, the twin said, "No."
2. When asked if Willard is the truth-teller, the twin again answered, "No."

Answer:

Bonus: What question could you ask either of the brothers, not knowing if he is a truth-teller or a liar, and always get a "No" reply?

Name ____________________________

Which Way to Jackson?

There are three brothers named Robert, Mike and Jason. Two brothers are liars. Only one brother is a truth-teller. You are standing at a fork in the road. There isn't a road sign. You need to go to Jackson. Use the facts given to deduce which road leads to Jackson.

Facts:

1. Robert tells you, "If you want to get to Jackson, you must take the left fork in the road."
2. Mike tells you, "My brother, Robert, is a liar. Do exactly the opposite as he tells you."
3. Jason tells you, "My brother, Mike, is a truth-teller, you should do as he says."

Answer:

Bonus: If two brothers are truth-tellers and only one brother is a liar, which fork in the road leads to Jackson?

Name ____________________

Truths, Lies and Half-Truths

There are three sisters named Alison, Bobbi and Cathy. One sister always tells the truth. One sister always lies. The third sister tells the truth half of the time and lies half of the time. Use the facts and construct a chart to deduce which sister is a truth-teller, which sister is a liar and which sister sometimes lies and sometimes tells the truth.

Facts:

1. When Bobbi lies, Cathy and Alison tell the truth.
2. When Cathy tells the truth, both Bobbi and Alison lie.
3. When Bobbi tells a lie, one of her sisters lies and one tells the truth.
4. When Alison tells the truth, one of her sisters lies and one tells the truth.
5. When Alison lies, one of her sisters lies and one tells the truth.
6. When Cathy tells the truth, one of her sisters lies and one tells the truth.

Answer:

Bonus: If given the exact same six facts, draw a chart to prove that each girl can tell the truth half of the time and lie half of the time.

Name ____________________

A Tangled Mess

There are four sisters named Darlene, Arlene, Judy and Jenny. One sister is an accurate truth-teller (understands what is true and always tells the truth). One sister is an inaccurate truth-teller (deluded and sees the opposite of the truth as being the truth). One sister is an accurate liar (knows the truth and always reports the opposite). One sister is an inaccurate liar (wants to tell lies, but thinks the opposite of the truth is the truth, so when she lies her answers are always the truth). Use the facts found below to eliminate all statements that contradict the facts to deduce which sister is an accurate truth-teller, which sister is an inaccurate truth-teller, which sister is an accurate liar and which sister is an inaccurate liar.

Facts:

1. When asked if Darlene was her sister, Jenny said, "No, she is my cousin and she is a liar."
2. When asked if she had an accurate truth-telling sister, Judy said, "Yes."
3. When asked if her sister Arlene tells lies, Darlene said, "Unknowingly my sister speaks falsely."

Accurate Truth-teller	Inaccurate Truth-teller	Accurate Liar	Inaccurate Liar
Darlene	Arlene	Judy	Jenny
Darlene	Judy	Arlene	Jenny
Darlene	Arlene	Jenny	Judy
Darlene	Judy	Jenny	Arlene
Darlene	Jenny	Judy	Arlene
Darlene	Jenny	Arlene	Judy
Arlene	Darlene	Judy	Jenny
Arlene	Judy	Darlene	Jenny
Arlene	Darlene	Jenny	Judy
Arlene	Judy	Jenny	Darlene
Arlene	Jenny	Judy	Darlene
Arlene	Jenny	Darlene	Judy
Judy	Darlene	Arlene	Jenny
Judy	Arlene	Darlene	Jenny
Judy	Darlene	Jenny	Arlene
Judy	Arlene	Jenny	Darlene
Judy	Jenny	Arlene	Darlene
Judy	Jenny	Darlene	Arlene
Jenny	Darlene	Arlene	Judy
Jenny	Darlene	Judy	Arlene
Jenny	Arlene	Judy	Darlene
Jenny	Arlene	Darlene	Judy
Jenny	Judy	Darlene	Arlene
Jenny	Judy	Arlene	Darlene

Answer:

Bonus: Make up all new clues for this puzzle so that each sister has a new identity.

Name ____________________

The Perfect Paper

Four students named Charlie, Jerry, Donna and Kim took a true-or-false test consisting of six questions. They answered the questions as follows:

	1	2	3	4	5	6
Charlie	T	F	T	F	F	T
Jerry	T	T	F	T	T	F
Donna	T	F	T	T	T	F
Kim	F	F	T	T	T	F

Use the facts and complete the chart found below to deduce which student had the perfect paper.

Facts:

1. No student received the same score on the test.
2. Charlie missed exactly half of the questions.

	Charlie	Kim	Donna	Jerry
If Jerry's paper was perfect. . .	-5			
If Kim's paper was perfect. . .				
If Donna's paper was perfect. . .				

Answer:

Bonus: If Jerry had the perfect score, who missed half of the questions?

Name ______________________

A Perfect Balance

In a certain sixth grade classroom there are twelve students. Use the facts and complete the chart found below to deduce how many girls and how many boys are in the class.

Facts:

1. If one boy moved away and the class got a new girl, there would be twice as many girls as boys.
2. If one girl moved away and the class got a new boy, there would be an equal number of boys and girls in the class.

Girls	Boys	Fact #1	Fact #2
11	1	12 Girls 0 Boys	10 Girls 2 Boys
10	2		
9	3		

Answer:

Bonus: In a class with a certain number of students, if the girls outnumber the boys three to one and there are eight more girls than boys, what is the total number of students in the class?

Name ____________________

How Old Are They?

Today the combined ages of three persons named Steve, Matthew and Anthony is seventy-one years. Use the facts and complete the chart found below to deduce the age of each.

Facts:

1. In three years, Anthony will be twice as old as Matthew.
2. When Matthew is half Anthony's age, Steve will be five.

If Steve is. . .	Matthew will be. . .	Anthony will be. . .
1		
2		
3		
4		
5		
6		
7		
8		
9		
10		
11		
12		

Answer:

Bonus: How old will Anthony be when Matthew is three times as old as Steve?

Name ______________________

Not Sixty-Five Yet!

Mary's grandfather isn't sixty-five yet. Use the facts and complete the chart found below to deduce the ages of Mary and her grandfather.

Facts:

1. The difference between Mary's age and her grandfather's age is 44 years.
2. The product of their ages is 1280 years.

Mary's Age	Grandfather's Age	Product
1	45	45
2	46	92
3		
4		
5		
6		
7		
8		
9		
10		
11		
12		
13		
14		
15		
16		
17		
18		
19		
20		

Answer:

Bonus: When Mary is exactly one-half her grandfather's age, what will be the product of their ages?

Name ______________________

My Three Sons

A woman has three handsome sons named Paul, George and Ringo. Use the facts and chart found below to deduce the ages of the three sons.

Facts:

1. The product of their ages is 36.
2. The sum of their ages is 13.
3. Ringo, the oldest son, likes to play basketball after school.

	Product	Sum
1, 1, 36		
1, 2, 18		
1, 3, 12		
1, 4, 9		
1, 6, 6		
2, 2, 9		
2, 3, 6		
3, 3, 4		

Answer:

Bonus: If the third clue had said, "The oldest sons like to play baseball after school," what would be the age of Ringo?

Name ____________________

Four Visitors

On Valentine's Day 1980, four boys named Alan, Bill, Cliff and Don visited their friend Gary. Alan went at 8:00. Bill went at 9:00. Cliff went at 10:00. Don went at 11:00. Use the facts and complete the chart found below to deduce whether each boy went in the a.m. or the p.m. (Cross off the possibilities that contradict the facts given below.)

Facts:

1. One or more boys visited Gary between Alan and Bill's visits.
2. Alan didn't visit Gary before Don visited Gary.
3. Cliff didn't visit Gary between Bill and Don.

Alan/8 a.m.	Bill/9 a.m.	Cliff/10 a.m.	Don/11 a.m.
Alan/8 a.m.	Cliff/10 a.m.	Don/11 a.m.	Bill /9 p.m.
Alan/8 a.m.	Cliff/10 a.m.	Bill/9 p.m.	Don/11 p.m.
Alan/8 a.m.	Don/11 a.m.	Bill/9 p.m.	Cliff/10 p.m.
Alan/8 a.m.	Bill/9 p.m.	Cliff/10 p.m.	Don/11 p.m.
Alan/8 p.m.	Bill/9 p.m.	Cliff/10 p.m.	Don/11 p.m.
Bill/9 a.m.	Cliff/10 a.m.	Don/11 a.m.	Alan/8 p.m.
Bill/9 a.m.	Don/11 a.m.	Alan/8 p.m.	Cliff/10 p.m.
Bill/9 a.m.	Alan/8 p.m.	Cliff/10 p.m.	Don/11 p.m.
Cliff/10 a.m.	Don/11 a.m.	Alan/8 p.m.	Bill/9 p.m.
Cliff/10 a.m.	Alan/8 p.m.	Bill/9 p.m.	Don/11 p.m.
Don/11 a.m.	Alan/8 p.m.	Bill/9 p.m.	Cliff/10 p.m.

Answer:

HAPPY VALENTINE'S DAY!

Bonus: What day of the week did the friends visit Gary?

Name ____________________

Just in Years

Justin has a sister named Mary. Neither child is a teenager yet. Use the facts and complete the chart found below to deduce the ages of Justin and his sister.

Facts:

1. Mary is three years younger than Justin.
2. If you add Mary's age to Justin's age times itself the total is 107.

Justin's Age	Justin's Age Squared	Mary's Age	Total
4	4 × 4 =	1	
5	5 × 5 =		
6	6 × 6 =		

Answer:

Bonus: In how many years will the square root of Mary's age plus Justin's age equal 159?

Name ____________________________

Birthday Candles Ablaze!

Great Grandmother Anne bought a candle for each year for her birthday cake. However, a series of misfortunes left Great Grandmother Anne with only one candle for every decade of her life, instead of every single year. Use the facts and complete the chart found below to deduce the age of Great Grandmother Anne.

Facts:

1. Half of the candles melted in the hot car before Great Grandmother Anne got them home. So she threw half of the candles away.
2. The day before Great Grandmother Anne's birthday, her great granddaughter, Mary, had a birthday. Mary borrowed fifteen of the remaining candles for her own cake.
3. Putting the candles on her cake, Great Grandmother Anne dropped twenty-one of the candles in the sink and got them wet, so she just tossed them in the trash.

Original Number of Candles	1/2 Box	-15	-21	Final #
60				
70				
80				
90				
100				

Answer:

Bonus: When Mary celebrates her twenty-fifth birthday, how old will Great Grandmother Anne be?

Name ____________________

Birds and Beasts

The Hanalei Zoo has eight more beasts than it has birds. Use the facts and complete the chart found below to deduce how many birds and how many beasts live in Hanalei Zoo.

Facts:

1. The total number of animal legs in the zoo is 104.
2. The total number of animal heads in the zoo is 32.

Number of Beasts	Legs	Heads	Number of of Birds	Legs	Heads	Total Legs	Total Heads
8	32	8	0	0	0	32	8
9							
10							
11							
12							
13							
14							
15							
16							
17							
18							
19							
20							
21							
22							
23							
24							

Answer:

Bonus: If there were exactly twice as many beasts as birds and 24 heads, how many total animals' legs would there be?

Name ____________________

Lots of Children

Three men named Jack, Jim and Joe have a total of nineteen children. Use the facts and complete the chart found below to deduce how many girls and how many boys each man has. (After you complete the chart, find the combination of children that totals nineteen and doesn't contradict any of the facts.)

Facts:

1. Jack has at least one girl and twice as many boys.
2. Jim has at least one girl and three times as many boys.
3. Joe has at least one girl and two more boys than girls.
4. The men each have a different number of girls.

Number of Girls	Jack's Boys	Total Children	Jim's Boys	Total Children	Joe's Boys	Total Children
1	2	3	3	4	3	4
2						
3						
4						
5						

Answer:

Bonus: If fact 4 wasn't there, what is the other possibility that doesn't contradict any of the first three facts?

Name ____________________

A Matter of Years

There is a man named Porter who has a son named Max. Porter and Max share the same birth date each year. Use the facts and construct a chart to deduce the age of father and son.

Facts:

1. Last year Porter was exactly twice as old as Max.
2. This year Porter's age is the reverse of Max's age. Example: 31 and 13.

Answer:

Bonus: How many years from now will Porter's and Max's ages be the reverse of each other?

Name ____________________

Questionable Twins

There are twin sisters named Amber and Grace. The sisters cannot answer questions; they can only ask them. One sister can only ask questions that will be answered "Yes." The other sister can only ask questions that can be answered "No." You meet one of the twins, and she asks you two questions. Use the questions and complete the chart found below to deduce if you are speaking with Amber or Grace and which sister asks which kind of questions.

Questions:

1. Do I have a sister named Grace?
2. Did I already ask you a question?

If Speaking	Your Reply to Question #1	Your Reply to Question #2
Amber/Yes		
Grace/Yes		
Amber/No		
Grace/No		

Answer:

Bonus: Write a question that can be answered "Yes" or "No" that neither of the sisters could ever ask.

Name ______________________________

The Party Animal

At a certain party there were ten people. Use the facts and complete the chart found below to determine how many party guests were men and how many were women.

Facts:

1. At least one guest is a man.
2. Given any two people at the party, at least one of them will always be a woman.

Guest #1	Man
Guest #2	
Guest #3	
Guest #4	
Guest #5	
Guest #6	
Guest #7	
Guest #8	
Guest #9	
Guest #10	

Answer:

Bonus: If there are two men and eight women at a party and you put all their names in a hat and draw out two names, what is the chance that you will draw out both men's names?

Name ______________________

Secret Word

The secret word has seven letters. Under each number below is a letter in the secret word plus two letters not found in the word. Use the fact and chart found below to deduce the secret word.

1	2	3	4	5	6	7
o	u	a	o	a	i	y
p	y	i	t	e	w	n
m	q	s	b	b	r	q

Fact:
1. There is only one letter repeated in the secret word.

Answer:

Bonus: If the fact had read, "There are no double letters in the secret word and you must unscramble the letters in the secret word," what would be the secret word?

Name ____________________

The School Chorus

Of the twenty children in the James Knight School chorus, there are an equal number of girls and boys. At Christmas the chorus members decided to wear red, white and green shirts. Use the facts and complete the chart found below to deduce how many girls wore green in the Christmas program. (First list the possibilities in each box, and then decide which of the possibilities do not contradict any of the facts.)

Facts:

1. Of the three color groups, each had a different number of members.
2. Twice as many girls wore red as boys wore green.
3. Four times as many girls wore white as boys wore red.
4. An equal number of girls wore red as boys wore white.
5. Three more boys wore green as girls wore green.
6. No girls wore green.

	Red	Green	White	Total
Boys				10
Girls				
Totals				20

Answer:

Bonus: Create your own color puzzle.

Name ______________________

Baseball Cards Galore!

There is a boy named Regan, who collects baseball cards. He has between 2500 and 3000 cards in his collection. Use the facts and divide to deduce how many cards are in his collection.

Facts:

1. When the total number of cards in his collection is divided by two, there is a remainder of one.
2. When the total number of cards in his collection is divided by three, there is a remainder of two.
3. When the total number of cards in his collection is divided by four, there is a remainder of three.
4. When the total number of cards in his collection is divided by five, there is a remainder of four.
5. When the total number of cards in his collection is divided by six, there is a remainder of five.
6. When the total number of cards in his collection is divided by seven, there is a remainder of six.
7. When the total number of cards in his collection is divided by eight, there is a remainder of seven.
8. When the total number of cards in his collection is divided by nine, there is a remainder of eight.
9. When the total number of cards in his collection is divided by ten, there is a remainder of nine.

Answer:

Bonus: Regan's sister, Nancy, collects dolls. If you divide the total number of dolls in her collection by two, three, four, five or six, you will always have a remainder of one. If you divide the total number of dolls by eleven, there isn't a remainder. How many dolls are in Nancy's collection? Hint: She had over 100 dolls.

Name ______________________

Mrs. Pole's Money Box

Mrs. Pole hid $1000 in a box in her bedroom a certain number of years ago. Use the facts and complete a chart to deduce how many years ago she hid the money and how much she has today.

Facts:

1. At the end of every third year she added 50% of the total amount of money in the box, to the box.
2. Today she discovered she cannot put an even amount of money in the box because she would need one half a penny.

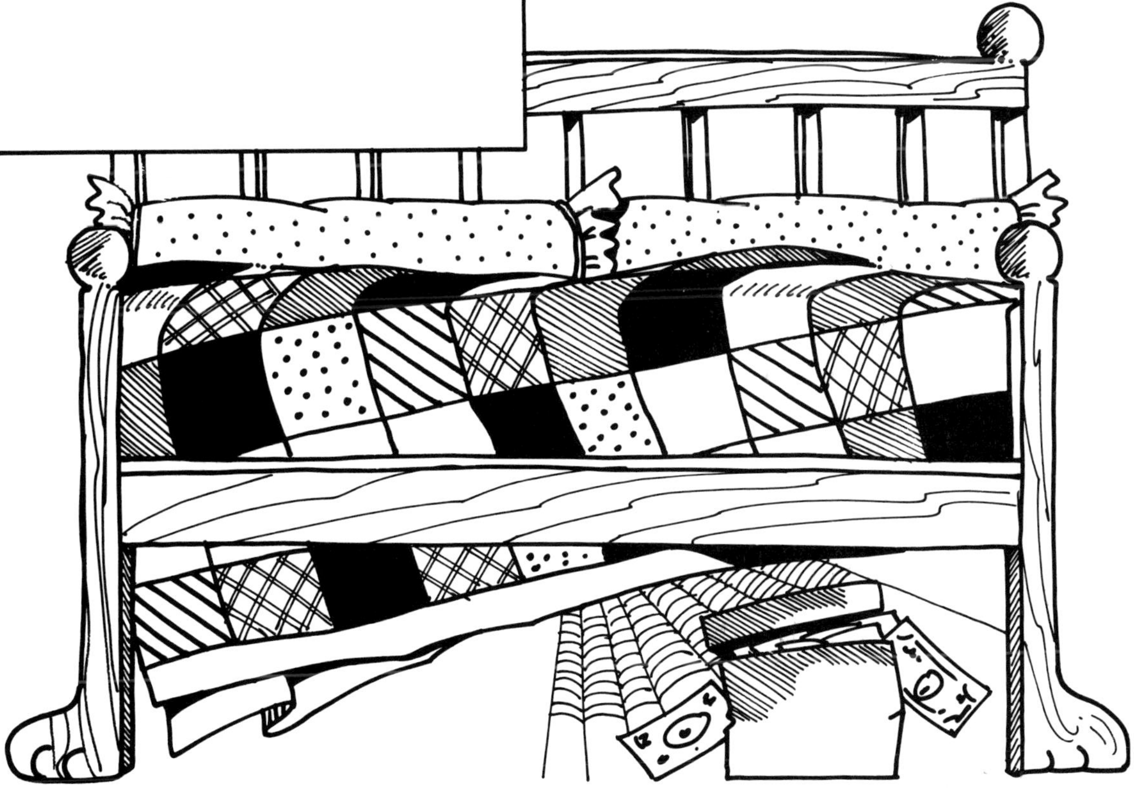

Answer:

Bonus: If Mrs. Pole decides to write herself a note for any fractional part of a cent and put it in the box until she needs a whole penny and then replaces the note with a coin, what will she have in her box in another three years?

Name ____________________

A Good Mistake

When Henry's father paid him his allowance, he accidentally gave his son dollars instead of cents and cents instead of dollars. For example, if Henry usually received one dollar and ten cents, this time he would have been paid ten dollars and one cent. Use the facts and complete the chart found below to deduce the usual amount of Henry's allowance. (Check one bill and one coin in each possibility and find the total. Which two reversed figures equal twice the smaller number when 15¢ is added to the larger number?)

Facts:

1. As usual, Henry's father gave him a single bill and a single coin.
2. If Henry's father had given him an additional 15¢, Henry would have received twice his normal allowance.

$10	$5	$1	50¢	25¢	10¢	5¢	1¢	Total
✓			✓					10.50
✓				✓				10.25
✓					✓			10.10

Answer:

Bonus: Henry saved one-half his weekly allowance for one year. When he withdrew the money from the bank, the teller gave him five bills and five coins. What were the bills and what were the coins?

Name ____________________

Nine Thousand Snails

At Crystal Bethany School 9919 snails were removed from the school's garden by the students. Use the facts and complete the chart below to deduce how many children attend Crystal Bethany School.

Facts:

1. Each child removed the same number of snails from the garden.
2. The number of snails that each child removed was eighteen more than the total number of students at the school.

Children	Snails	Product
50	50 (+18) = 68	3400
60		
70		

Answer:

Bonus: If you were not given fact 2, give three other correct answers for this puzzle.

Name ____________________

Jelly Bean Mix

At Betty's Candy Shop you can buy her special mixed jelly beans for 45¢ per pound. Betty mixes a certain number of pounds of 25¢ jelly beans with a certain number of pounds of 95¢ jelly beans to make a 100-pound mixture. Use the fact and complete the chart found below to deduce what percentage of each kind of jelly beans she uses in the 100-pound mixture.

Fact:

1. For every 100 pounds she mixes, she spends $4.60 more for inexpensive jelly beans than she spends for expensive ones.

100-Pound Combinations	25¢	95¢	Difference
70%/30%	70 × 25¢ =	30 × 95¢ =	
75%/25%			
80%/20%			

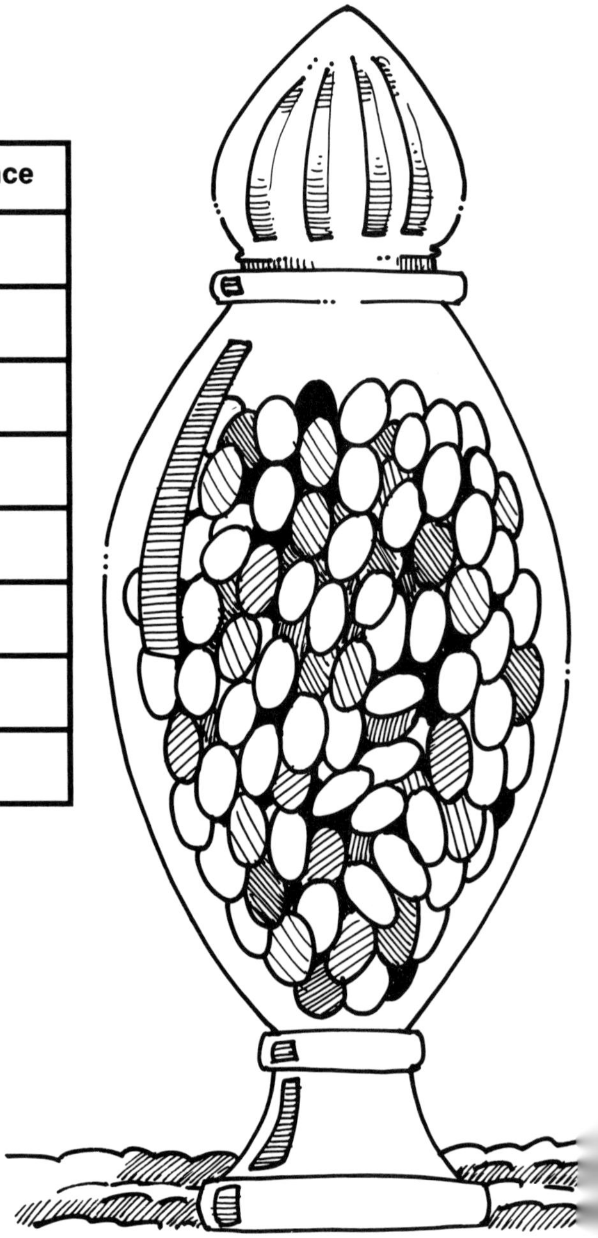

Answer:

Bonus: How much profit does Betty make on each pound of jelly bean mixture she sells?

Name ______________________

Answer Key

Beautiful, Blond and Intelligent Page 1
Yvette is the blond, beautiful and intelligent sister.
Steps to deduce the answer:
Fact 1 tells us that Wendy and Zelda have red hair.
Fact 2 doesn't give us a clue at this time so skip down to the next clue.
Fact 3 tells us that Wendy and Yvette have the same hair color (which we know to be false) or that Zelda and Yvette are the only two beautiful sisters and Virginia has brown hair (which we now know must be true). We can also list the fact that Virginia and Wendy are not beautiful.
Fact 2 tells us that Virginia and Yvette are the only two intelligent sisters or Virginia is beautiful (which we know to be false). So Virginia and Yvette are the intelligent sisters and Wendy and Zelda are not intelligent.
We now can deduce from the chart that Yvette does not have red or brown hair (she must be the blond); she is also both beautiful and intelligent.
Bonus: Wendy

Let's Dine Out! Page 2
Mrs. Brown, Mr. Brown, Mrs. Green, Mr. Green, Mrs. White, Mr. White
Steps to deduce the answer:
Fact 2 tells us that each husband did not sit directly across the table from his wife.
Fact 1 tells us that each husband sat directly across the table from his wife (which we know to be false) or each husband sat on the left of his wife (which we know must be true).
Now we just have to place the couples so that Mrs. Brown is across from Mr. Green or Mrs. Green and since each man will sit across from a woman, Mrs. Brown must be sitting directly across the table from Mr. Green. The rest of the puzzle is easy.
Bonus: No, it is not possible.

What's My Line? Page 3
Mike, writer; wife, lawyer; mother, doctor; son, teacher
Steps to deduce the answer:
Fact 1 tells us that the lawyer and doctor are both men or both women. Cross off all possibilities that list a man lawyer and a woman doctor or a woman lawyer and a man doctor. (There are 16 of these.)
Fact 2 tells us that the teacher and writer are father and son or husband and wife. So cross off any possibilities that the mother is a teacher or a writer. (There are 4 of these.)
Fact 3 tells us that the writer and lawyer are husband and wife or grandmother and grandson. Cross off the possibilities that contradict this fact. (There are 2 of these.)
Fact 4 tells us that Mike is not married to the doctor which elminates one of the last two possibilities, leaving the answer.
Bonus: 16 out of 24 or 66.66%

A Triple Date Page 4
Eric & Jamie; Betty & Tom; Beth & Tim
Steps to deduce the answer:
Fact 1 tells us that Eric is dating Betty or Jamie; therefore, we can cross off the two possibilities that Eric is dating Beth. Eric or Tom is dating Betty; therefore, Tim is not dating Betty, and we can cross off the two possibilities that Tim is dating Betty.
Fact 2 tells us that Tom is dating Betty or Beth; therefore we can cross off the two possibilities that Tom is dating Jamie. The second part of fact 2 states that either Tim is dating Betty (which we know now to be false), or Tom is dating Betty (which must be true). Now we know one couple is Tom/Betty.
Fact 1 tells us that if Tom is dating Betty (which we know to be true), that Eric is dating Jamie. Now we know two couples, Tom/Betty and Eric/Jamie, which leaves us the third couple Tim/Beth.
Bonus: Yes, Tim & Betty

Hawaii Bound Page 5
Diane and Linda are going to Hawaii. Naomi, youngest and middle-sized; Linda, oldest and shortest; Diane, middle-aged and tallest.
Steps to deduce the answer:
Fact 1 tells us that Naomi is the youngest or the oldest; therefore, we can cross off the possibility that she is middle-aged. Diane is the tallest or the shortest; therefore, we can cross off the possibility that she is middle-sized.
Fact 2 tells us that Linda is the tallest or shortest; therefore, we can cross off the possibility that she is middle-sized. Linda is the youngest or the oldest; therefore, we can cross off the possibility that she is middle-aged. Now we know from possibilities that have been eliminated that Diane is middle-aged and Naomi is middle-sized.
Fact 3 states that if Diane is the middle-aged sister (which we have proved to be true), that Naomi is the youngest, which leaves Linda to be the oldest.
Fact 1 tells us that if Naomi is the youngest (which we have proved to be true), that Diane is the tallest.
Bonus: Linda

Four Friends Page 6
Mon. Kathy & Nancy; Tues. David & Jay; Wed. Kathy & David; Thurs. David & Nancy; Fri. Kathy & Jay
Steps to deduce the answer:
Fact 1 cannot be used for a clue yet; go on to fact 2.
Fact 2 tells us that on Monday Kathy and Nancy or Nancy and Jay stayed to help; therefore, we can cross off the other four possibilities on Monday.
Fact 3 tells us that on Friday Kathy and David or Kathy and Jay stayed to help; therefore, we can cross off the other four possibilities on Friday.
Fact 4 tells us that Kathy and Nancy must have stayed because the other possibility (Nancy & Jay) is boy/girl.
Fact 5 tells us that on Wednesday Kathy and David or David and Jay stayed to help; therefore, we can cross off the other four possibilities under Wednesday.
Fact 6 is not a clue at this time so go back to fact 1.
Fact 1 states that neither of the girls stayed to help the teacher two days in a row; therefore, neither Kathy nor Nancy stayed on Tuesday (because we have proved that they stayed on Monday). Cross off the five possibilities under Tuesday that include a girl, and we are left with the only possible combination for Tuesday, David and Jay. Since we know from the directions that a different pair of children stayed each day, David and Jay could not have stayed on Wednesday; therefore, Kathy and David stayed on Wednesday. They could not have stayed on Friday; therefore, Kathy and Jay stayed on Friday.
Fact 1 tells us that if Kathy stayed on Wednesday, she could not have stayed on Thursday; therefore, cross off the three possibilities that Kathy stayed on Thursday.
Fact 6 tells us that Jay could not stay on Thursday or Kathy could not stay on Friday (which we have proven to be true); therefore, Jay could not stay on Thursday. Cross off the two possibilities left under Thursday that include Jay; therefore, David and Nancy stayed on Thursday. Now you have all the facts you need to solve this puzzle!
Bonus: No. Fact 1 is how we know that David & Jay stayed on Tuesday, and most of the other facts are based on that condition.

Last Name, Please Page 7
Kathy Joe; Helen Evans; Carole Mac
Steps to deduce the answer:
Fact 1 tells us that Kathy is not Miss Evans; therefore, cross off the two possibilities that Kathy's last name is Evans.
Fact 2 tells us that Carole's last name is either Evans or Mac; therefore, cross off the two possibilities that her last name is Joe. Helen's last name is Mac or Evans; therefore, cross off the two possibilities that Helen's last name is Joe.
Fact 3 tells us that Helen is not Miss Mac; therefore, cross off the two possibilities that Helen's last name is Mac. Now by the process of elimination we know that Carole's last name is Mac.
Fact 2 tells us that if Carole's last name is Mac (which we have proven), then Helen's last name is Evans. That leaves the last name of Joe for Kathy.
Bonus: Carole

What's for Lunch, Boys? Page 8
Adam, burger/soda
Bob, pizza/shake
Carl, salad/milk
Steps to deduce the answer:
Fact 1 tells us that either Adam or Carl drank the soda; therefore, cross off the possibilities that Bob drank the soda. Bob or Adam drank the shake; therefore, cross off the three possibilities that Carl had the shake. Adam had a soda or a shake; therefore, cross off the possibilities that Adam drank milk.

Fact 2 tells us that Carl had salad or burger; therefore, cross off the possibilities that Carl had pizza. Adam had a burger or pizza; therefore, cross off the possibilities that he had salad.
Fact 3 tells us that the combination of a burger and shake is impossible; therefore, cross off all burger/shake combinations.
Fact 4 tells us that Bob had burger/milk or pizza/shake; therefore, cross off all other combinations under Bob.
Fact 5 tells us that Adam didn't have pizza or milk; therefore, cross off any combination that has pizza or milk under Adam. The process of elimination tells us that Adam had a burger and soda.
Fact 1 tells us that if Adam drank a soda (which we have proven to be true), that Bob had a shake; therefore, we know that Bob had pizza/shake, leaving the salad/milk for Carl.
Bonus: They ate the same lunches.

The Dating Game Page 9

	Larry	Curly	Moe
Anna			•
Anita		•	
Andrea	•		

Steps to deduce the answer:
Fact 1 tells us that Anita was with Curly or Larry; therefore, cross off the possibility that Anita was with Moe. Larry was with Anita or Andrea; therefore, cross off the possibility that Larry was with Anna. Anna or Anita was with Curly; therefore, cross off the possibility that Andrea was with Curly.
Fact 2 tells us that Moe was with Anita or Anna; therefore, cross off the possibility that Moe was with Andrea. The process of elimination tells us that Moe was with Anna. If Moe was with Anna (which we have proven to be true), then Anita was with Curly, leaving Andrea/Larry as the last combination.
Bonus: same dates

No Clowning Around Page 10
Mrs. White

	Mr. Sue	Mrs. Sue	Mr. Red	Mrs. Red	Mr. White	Mrs. White
ladybug	•					
devil			•			
angel				•		
lion					•	
Shake-speare		•				
clown						•

Steps to deduce the answer:
Fact 1 tells us that the Reds or the Whites came as devil and angel; therefore, the Sues did not come as devil and angel.
Fact 2 tells us that Mr. Sue was a ladybug or devil; since we know Mr. Sue did not come as the devil, he was the ladybug. Mrs. Sue was an angel or Shakespeare, and we have proven she was not the angel; therefore, Mrs. Sue was Shakespeare.
Fact 3 tells us that Mr. Red was a lion or a devil; therefore, cross off all other possibilities under Mr. Red. Mrs. White was not the ladybug (we have proven that Mr. Sue was the ladybug); therefore, we know that Mr. Red was the devil and Mr. White was the lion.
Fact 1 tells us that if Mr. Red was the devil (which we have proven), then Mrs. Red was the angel. Through the process of elimination we know that Mrs. White was dressed in the clown suit and is the thief!
Bonus: Mr. White

They All Have Wheels Page 11

	Chris	Victor	Brad
bike	•		
scooter		•	
skates			•

Steps to deduce the answer:
Fact 1 tells us that Chris rode a bike or skated; therefore, cross off the possibility that Chris had a scooter. Brad skated or rode his bike; therefore, Brad didn't have the scooter either. We already can deduce that Victor rode the scooter.
Fact 2 tells us that if Victor had a scooter. Chris rode his bike. Through a process of elimination we are left with Brad/skates.
Bonus: Answers will vary.

What Color Hat? Page 12
Beth's hat is blue.
Steps to deduce the answer:
If either child sees the only orange hat, he/she would know that the color of his/her own hat was blue.
Fact 1 tells us that John doesn't see Beth wearing the only orange hat; therefore, Beth must be wearing a blue hat.
Fact 2 tells us that Beth doesn't see John wearing the only orange hat; therefore, John must be wearing a blue hat, too.
Bonus: If John's hat was orange, Beth knew she was seeing the only orange hat; therefore, her hat had to be blue. If John's hat was blue, Beth needed the fact that John couldn't name the color of his hat. If John didn't see the only orange hat, he wouldn't know the color of his hat; therefore, Beth knew she was wearing a blue hat.

Fives Hats Page 13
Amy, yellow; Sarah, yellow; Eric, pink
Steps to deduce the answer:
If Eric saw that the girls were wearing both of the yellow hats, he knew the color of his hat was pink.
Bonus: Eric knew he was wearing a pink hat because he and Sarah could see one of the two yellow hats (worn by Amy), and Sarah didn't know the color of her hat; therefore, Eric knew he wasn't wearing the other yellow hat.

Black and White Hats Page 14
Answers may vary depending on how much the children assume from previous answers given. The chart found below is based on what Mike and Max see and on assumptions made by Nancy regarding what the other two children state. If, however, the second child Max made assumptions regarding the color of his hat based on what Mike said, the chart will look very different. There are many acceptable answers for this chart.

What Each Child Would Know

	Fact 1	Fact 2	Fact 3
MIKE/BLACK MAX/BLACK NANCY/BLACK	?	?	?
MIKE/WHITE MAX/BLACK NANCY/BLACK	?	?	I Know
MIKE/BLACK MAX/WHITE NANCY/BLACK	?	?	I Know
MIKE/BLACK MAX/BLACK NANCY/WHITE	?	?	?
MIKE/BLACK MAX/WHITE NANCY/WHITE	I Know	?	I Know
MIKE/WHITE MAX/BLACK NANCY/WHITE	?	I Know	I Know
MIKE/WHITE MAX/WHITE NANCY/BLACK	?	?	I Know

Six Hats Page 15
Julie's hat was red. Since all three girls could see a red hat, at least two girls must be wearing a red hat. If Julie could see only one red hat, she knew that she was wearing a red hat, or the sister wearing the red hat would see only green hats. Therefore, one of her sisters is wearing red and one is wearing green.
Bonus: Janet, red; Julie, red; Jill, green. If Jill was wearing a green hat, Janet and Julie each saw the red hat worn by the other and knew the color of her hat. Jill could deduce that she had to be wearing a green hat or neither of her sisters would have been able to tell the color of her own hat.

The Prize Box Page 16
Box 2 contains the prize.
Box 2 says one box is empty and one box contains the prize which we know to be true; therefore, the note on box 1 must be false and box 1 cannot contain the prize.
Bonus: Box 1 contains the prize.

Three Boxes Page 17
Box 1 contains the prize.
Box 1 and box 2 agree that the first box is empty. Since there can only be one true note, box three must contain the only true statements. If the messages on box 1 and box 2 are false, box 1 contains the prize.
Bonus: If all the statements are true, box 2 contains the prize. All three statements cannot be false or there would be a prize in box 1 and box 3.

All True or All Lies Page 18
Box 2, all statements are false.

What would be in box if:	Box 1	Box 2	Box 3
T/T/T	P	E	P
F/F/F	E	P	E

Bonus: Box 2 definitely doesn't have a prize. Boxes 1 and 3 say the same thing, and since there is only one true note, the prize must be in 1 or 3.

Pick a Box, Any Box! Page 19
The prize is in the first box. Boxes 1 and 4 both claim to contain the prize. Since only one box contains a prize, one of the boxes must contain the only false statement. Boxes 2 and 3 must contain true statements. Box 3 says the prize is in box 1 and it is a true statement; therefore, the prize must be in box 1.
Bonus: Answers will vary.

Say That Again Page 20
The prize is in box 4. Statement on box 1 is false. All other possibilities have contradictions.

	Box 1	Box 2	Box 3	Box 4
If 1 is F...	E	E	E	P
If 2 is F...	P/E	P/E	E	E/P
If 3 is F...	P	P/E	P/E	E/P
If 4 is F...	P/E	E	E	E/P

Bonus: Answers will vary.

George's Rabbits Page 21
Either answer, black or white, is acceptable. If George looked inside the first box and saw a black rabbit (the only true statement), he would know that the notes on the other two boxes could not be true. Since he looked and saw that the spotted rabbit was in the third box (a false statement), the white rabbit must be in the second box (the other false statement). If George looked inside the first box and saw a white rabbit (a false statement) and there was a spotted rabbit in box 3 (another false statement), the black rabbit was inside the second box (the only true statement).
Bonus: Box 2 contains the white rabbit.

Suzi's Rabbits Page 22
box 1, brown; box 2, white; box 3, gray
If Suzi sees the brown rabbit in the first box, she knows that the note on box 1 is false, and since the note on box 2 claims to contain the brown rabbit, we know that statements 1 and 2 are the false statements; therefore, the note on box 3 must be true.

	Box 1	Box 2	Box 3
T/F/F	White	Gray	Brown
F/T/F	Not W Gray	Brown	Not G White
F/F/T	Not W Brown	Not B White	Gray

Bonus: Box 3 contains the brown rabbit. If Suzi knows box 3 contains a gray rabbit, box 3 cannot contain a gray rabbit also; therefore box 3 must be the second false statement and box 1 must contain a true statement and a white rabbit.

Pete's Rabbits Page 23
Box 1, gray; box 2, brown; box 3, white; box 4, black.
If Pete looked inside box 4 and saw the black rabbit, he knew that the black rabbit was not in box 1. Since box 1 contained the only false statement, the other three boxes had to contain the color rabbit indicated by the note attached to each.
Bonus: Answers will vary.

Bryan's Rabbits Page 24
Box 1, brown; box 2, white; box 3, gray; box 4, black
If Bryan saw a brown rabbit inside box 1, he knew that the message on the box was true; therefore, the black rabbit was in the last box. Therefore, the message on the last box was false and since the message on the second box said that the brown rabbit was in the last box (which we have proven to be false), we know that the message on box 2 is the other false message. The messages on box 1 and box 3 are true.
Bonus: Box 3

Barbara and Joann Page 25
You are addressing Barbara the truth-teller.
Steps to deduce the answer:
Barbara the truth-teller would answer both questions "Yes."
Barbara the liar would answer the first question "Yes," and the second question "No."
Joann the truth-teller would answer both questions "No."
Joann the liar would answer the first question "Yes," and the second question "No."
Bonus:Answers will vary. One possible solution is to ask, "Is Barbara the truth-teller your sister?" Barbara the liar is the only one that could answer that question "Yes."

You Decide Page 26
Lee is the truth-teller and patient; George is a liar and a doctor.

If...	Fact 1	Fact 2	Fact 3
Lee t-t/doc Geo l/pat	No	No	No
Lee l/doc Geo t-t/pat	Yes	Yes	No
Lee t-t/doc Geo l/doc	Yes	Yes	Yes
Lee l/doc Geo t-t/doc	No	No	Yes

Bonus: The doctor would still be the liar, but his name would be Lee. George the truth-teller would be the patient.

Arrest That Twin! Page 27
Arrest the first speaker; he is Paul and a liar. Peter is the second speaker and he is lying this time.

If...	Reply to Question 1	Reply to Question 2
Peter/t-t Paul/lying	Yes	Yes
Peter/lying Paul/lying	No	Yes
Peter/lying Paul/t-t	No	No
Paul/t-t Peter/lying	No	No
Paul/lying Peter t-t	Yes	Yes
Paul/lying Peter/lying	Yes	No

Bonus: Arrest the second speaker which is Paul. Both brothers are lying in this case, too.

Double Whammy Page 28
You are addressing Doug.

	Fact #1 Answer	Fact #2 Answer
Tom acc/t-t	Yes	No
Jeff inacc/t-t	No	Yes
Doug acc/liar	Yes	Yes
Jack inacc/liar	No	Yes

Bonus: Jeff

Willard and Gene Page 29
You are addressing Gene the truth-teller.

If...	Response Question 1	Response Question 2
Willard/ Truth-teller & Gene/Liar	Yes	Yes
Gene/Truth-Teller & Willard/Liar	No	No
Gene/Liar & Willard/ Truth-Teller	Yes	No
Willard/Liar Yes & Gene/Truth-Teller	No	Yes

Bonus: Are you a liar?

Which Way to Jackson? Page 30
Mike and Jason agree that the right road leads to Jackson. Since two brothers are liars, the other brother, Robert, must be the truth-teller. Therefore, the left road leads to Jackson.
Bonus: right road

Truths, Lies and Half-Truths Page 31
Cathy always tells the truth. Bobbi always lies. Alison tells the truth half of the time and lies half of the time.

	Alison	Bobbi	Cathy
Fact 1	T	L	T
Fact 2	L	L	T
Fact 3	(L) or T	L	(T) or L
Fact 4	T	(L) or T	(T) or L
Fact 5	L	(L) or T	(T) or L
Fact 6	(T) or L	(L) or T	T

Bonus:

	Alison	Bobbi	Cathy
Fact 1	T	L	T
Fact 2	L	L	T
Fact 3	(T) or L	L	(L) or T
Fact 4	T	(T) or L	(L) or T
Fact 5	L	(T) or L	(L) or T
Fact 6	(L) or T	(T) or L	T

A Tangled Mess Page 32
Darlene, accurate truth-teller; Arlene, inaccurate truth-teller; Jenny, accurate liar; Judy, inaccurate liar
Steps to deduce the answer:
Fact 1 tells us that Jenny is either an inaccurate truth-teller or an accurate liar because she said that Darlene was her cousin (we know she is her sister). Cross off all possibilities that Jenny is an accurate truth-teller or an inaccurate liar. Since we know that Jenny doesn't speak the truth, the second part of her statement (Darlene is a liar) must also be false. Cross off all possibilities that Darlene is an inaccurate truth-teller or an accurate liar.
Fact 3 tells us that Arlene is the inaccurate truth-teller because we know Darlene speaks the truth, and the sister that would "unknowingly speak falsely" is the inaccurate truth-teller. Cross off all possibilities that Arlene is not the inaccurate truth-teller.
Fact 2 tells us that Judy is not the accurate truth-telling sister. If she were the accurate truth-teller, she would not say she had an accurate truth-telling sister; therefore, cross off the possibilities that Judy is the accurate truth-teller.
Process of elimination leaves only one possibility and the answer.
Bonus: Answers will vary.

The Perfect Paper Page 33
Donna had the perfect paper.

	Charlie	Kim	Donna	Jerry
If Jerry's paper was perfect. . .	-5	-3	-2	-0
If Kim's paper was perfect. . .	-4	-0	-1	-3
If Donna's paper was perfect. . .	-3	-1	-0	-2

Bonus: Kim

A Perfect Balance Page 34
7 girls and 5 boys

Girls	Boys	Fact #1	Fact #2
11	1	12 G and 0 B	10 G and 2 B
10	2	11 G and 1 B	9 G and 3 B
9	3	10 G and 2 B	8 G and 4 B
8	4	9 G and 3 B	7 G and 5 B
7	5	8 G and 4 B	6 G and 6 B
6	6	7 G and 5 B	5 G and 7 B
5	7	6 G and 6 B	4 G and 8 B
4	8	5 G and 7 B	3 G and 9 B

Bonus: 12 girls and 4 boys, total 16

How Old Are They? Page 35
Steve, 2; Matthew, 22; Anthony, 47
Steps to deduce the answer:
Fact 1 tells us that in three years Anthony will be twice as old as Matthew.
Fact 2 tells us that when Anthony is twice Matthew's age, Steve will be five; therefore, Steve will be five in three years. Now we know that Steve is two years old today. In three years Steve will be 5, and the total of all three persons will be 71 plus 9 years (each will be three years older) or 80. If we subtract five years for Steve's age, we are left with 75 years. If Anthony will be twice Matthew's age, we know he will be 50 and Matthew will be 25. Since this is the age of the persons in three years, we must back up on the chart to discover their ages today.
Bonus: 55

Not Sixty-Five Yet! Page 36
Mary, 20; grandfather, 64

Mary's Age	Grandfather's Age	Product
1	45	45
2	46	92
3	47	141
4	48	192
5	49	245
6	50	300
7	51	357
8	52	416
9	53	477
10	54	540
11	55	605
12	56	672
13	57	741
14	58	812
15	59	885
16	60	960
17	61	1037
18	62	1116
19	63	1197
20	64	1280

Bonus: 3872 (44 x 88)

My Three Sons Page 37
Ringo, 9; Paul, 2; George, 2
Steps to deduce the answer:
Fact 1 gives us the factors listed in the first column.
Fact 2 tells us the sum of the ages is 13; therefore, the boys must be 1,6, and 6 or 2,2 and 9.
Fact 3 tells us that the oldest son likes to play basketball; therefore, the oldest of the boys cannot be two boys (twins).
Bonus: Ringo would be 1 and the twins would be 6.

Four Visitors Page 38
Bill, 9 a.m.; Don, 11 a.m.; Alan, 8 p.m.; Cliff, 10 p.m.
Steps to deduce the answer:
Fact 1 tells us that Gary had at least one visitor between Alan and Bill; therefore, cross off all possibilities that Alan's visit was just before or just after Bill's.
Fact 2 tells us that Alan's visit didn't come before Don's visit; therefore, cross off all possibilities that Alan went before Don.
Fact 3 tells us that Cliff's visit cannot be between Bill's and Don's; therefore, cross off any possibilities that Cliff's visit was between Bill's and Don's.
Process of elmination leaves the only possibility.
Bonus: Thursday

Just in Years Page 39
Justin, 10; Mary, 7

Justin's Age	Justin's Age Squared	Mary's Age	Total
4	4 × 4 = 16	1	17
5	5 × 5 = 25	2	27
6	6 × 6 = 36	3	39
7	7 × 7 = 49	4	53
8	8 × 8 = 64	5	69
9	9 × 9 = 81	6	87
10	10 × 10 = 100	7	107
11	11 × 11 = 121	8	129
12	12 × 12 = 144	9	153

Bonus: 5 years (Mary 12, 12 × 12 = 144 + 15 = 159)

Birthday Candles Ablaze! Page 40
90 years old

Candles	1/2 Box	-15	-21	Final #
60	30	15	-6	-6
70	35	20	-1	-1
80	40	25	4	4
90	45	30	9	9
100	50	35	14	14

Bonus: It will be the day before Great Grandmother Anne's 100th birthday; she will be 99.

Birds and Beasts Page 41
20 beasts and 12 birds

Number of Beasts	Legs	Heads	Number of Birds	Legs	Heads	Total Heads	Total
8	32	8	0	0	0	32	8
9	36	9	1	2	1	38	10
10	40	10	2	4	2	44	12
11	44	11	3	6	3	50	14
12	48	12	4	8	4	56	16
13	52	13	5	10	5	62	18
14	56	14	6	12	6	68	20
15	60	15	7	14	7	74	22
16	64	16	8	16	8	80	24
17	68	17	9	18	9	86	26
18	72	18	10	20	10	92	28
19	76	19	11	22	11	98	30
20	80	20	12	24	12	104	32
21	84	21	13	26	13	110	34
22	88	22	14	28	14	116	36
23	92	23	15	30	15	122	38
24	96	24	16	32	16	128	40

Bonus: 80 legs

Lots of Children Page 42
Jack, 1 girl and 2 boys; Jim, 2 girls and 6 boys; Joe, 3 girls and 5 boys

Number of Girls	Jack's Boys	Total Children	Jim's Boys	Total Children	Joe's Boys	Total Children
1	2	3	3	4	3	4
2	4	6	6	8	4	6
3	6	9	9	12	5	8
4	8	12	12	16	6	10
5	10	15	15	20	7	12

Bonus: Jack, 1 girl and 2 boys; Jim, 1 girl and 3 boys; Joe, 5 girls and 7 boys

A Matter of Years Page 43
Porter; 73; Max 37

If Porter Is	Max Is	Porter Last Year	Max Last Year
31	13	30	12
41	14	40	13
42	24	41	23
51	15	50	14
52	25	51	24
53	35	52	34
61	16	60	15
62	26	61	25
63	36	62	35
71	17	70	16
72	27	71	26
73	37	72	36

Hint: Father and son have to have at least a twenty-year difference in their ages, and the father must be at least 31.
Bonus: In 11 years Porter will be 84 and Max will be 48.

Questionable Twins Page 44
You are speaking with Amber the "Yes" sister.

If Speaking	Your Reply to Question #1	Your Reply to Question #2
Amber/Yes	If you are Amber, Yes. If you are Grace, No.	Yes
Grace/Yes	If you are Amber, Yes. If you are Grace, No.	Yes
Amber/No	If you are Amber, Yes. If you are Grace, No.	Yes
Grace/No	If you are Amber, Yes, If you are Grace, No.	Yes

Bonus: Am I the type who could ask a question and expect to get a negative response?
Hint: If "Yes" sister asked this question, she would get a "No." If "No" sister asked this question, she would get a "Yes."

The Party Animal Page 45
1 man and 9 women. If the 1 man represents one member of any pair, the rest must all be women.
Bonus: 2 times out of 90 draws you should get a combination of two men's names. 56 times out of 90 you will get both women's names. 32 times out of 90 you will get one man's name and one woman's name.

Secret Word Page 46
mystery
Bonus: punster

The School Chorus Page 47
Zero girls wore green.
Boys: 1 red, 3 green, 6 white
Girls: 6 red, 0 green, 4 white
Steps to deduce the answer:
Facts 1-5 do not give us a clue yet; go on to fact 6.
Fact 6 tells us that zero girls wore green; therefore, put zero on the chart for girls in green.
Fact 5 tells us that three more boys wore green than girls; therefore, put 3 on the chart for boys in green.
Fact 2 tells us that twice as many girls wore red as boys wore green; therefore, put 6 on the chart for girls in red.
Fact 4 tells us that the number of boys wearing white was the same as the number of girls wearing red; therefore, put 6 on the chart for boys in white.
The directions tell us that there is an equal number of girls and boys. Since we have proven that six girls wore red and zero girls wore green, we know that four girls must have worn white.
Fact 3 tells us that four times as many girls wore white as boys wore red; therefore, put 1 on the chart for boys in red.
Fact 2 tells us that twice as many girls wore red as boys wore green; therefore, put 3 on the chart for boys in green.
Bonus: Answers will vary.

Baseball Cards Galore! Page 48
2519 baseball cards
Hint: Begin with first number bigger than 2500 that when divided by 9 leaves a remainder of 8. List every ninth number after that until you find one that works.
Bonus: 121 dolls

Mrs. Pole's Money Box Page 49
15 years ago. She has $11,390.62 ½ today.

Year	Has	Added	Total
1	0	$1000	$1000
3	$1000	$500	$1500
6	$1500	$750	$2250
9	$2250	$1125	$3375
12	$3375	$1687.50	$5062.50
15	$5062.50	$2531.25	$7593.75
18	$7593.75	$3796.87½	$11390.62½
		$5695.3125	$17,085.937

Bonus: $17,085.93 and a note for ¾¢

A Good Mistake Page 50
$5.10 allowance; received $10.05

$10	$5	$1	50¢	25¢	10¢	5¢	1¢	Total
✓			✓					10.50
✓				✓				10.25
✓					✓			10.10
✓						✓		10.05
✓							✓	10.01
	✓		✓					5.50
	✓			✓				5.25
	✓				✓			5.10
	✓					✓		5.05
	✓						✓	5.01
		✓	✓					1.50
		✓		✓				1.25
		✓			✓			1.10
		✓				✓		1.05
		✓					✓	1.01

Bonus: $132.60: 2/$50 bills 1/$20 bill; 1/$10 bill; 1/$1 bill; 3/50¢ pieces and 2/nickels

Nine Thousand Snails Page 51
91 students; 109 snails

Children	Snails	Product
50	68	3400
60	78	4680
70	88	6160
80	98	7840
90	108	9720
91	109	9919

Bonus: 1 student collected 9919 snails; 9919 students each collected 1 snail; 109 students each collected 91 snails.

Jelly Bean Mix Page 52
83 lbs. at 25¢; 17 lbs. at 95¢

100-Pound Combinations	25¢	95¢	Difference
70%/30%	17.50	28.50	$11.00
75%/25%	18.75	23.75	$5.00
80%/20%	20.00	19.00	$1.00
81%/19%	20.25	18.05	$2.20
82%/18%	20.50	17.10	$3.40
83%/17%	20.75	16.15	$4.60

Bonus: $8.10 per lb., 100 lbs. and 8 1/10¢ per lb.

BONUS AWARD CERTIFICATE

To______________________________

____

From____________________________

____

Logic Genius Award!!!

To____

From______________________________________

Logic Expert

To ______________________

From ______________________

☆☆☆☆☆☆☆☆☆☆☆☆☆☆☆☆☆

Award Certificate

☆☆☆☆

To ______________________

From ______________________

EXTRA EFFORT!!!

TO ______________________

FROM ______________________

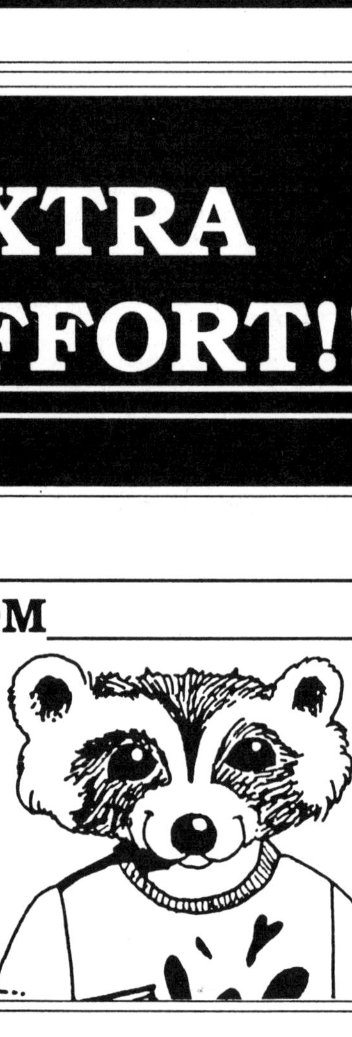

LOGIC WHIZ KID!!!!

To ______________________

From ______________________